# TOXIC WASTE

BY
SUSAN DUDLEY GOLD

CRESTWOOD HOUSE
New York

Collier Macmillan Canada
Toronto

Maxwell Macmillan International Publishing Group
New York  Oxford  Singapore  Sydney

**Library of Congress Cataloging-in-Publication Data**
Gold, Susan Dudley.
　　Toxic waste / by Susan Dudley Gold. — 1st ed.
　　　　p. cm. — (Earth alert)
　　Includes bibliographical references.
　　Summary: Discusses the causes and tragic effects of chemical waste pollution, efforts to reverse existing and prevent future damage, laws regulating the disposal of toxic wastes, and how you can get involved in the fight against pollution.
　　1. Hazardous wastes—Environmental aspects—Juvenile literature. 2. Hazardous wastes—Environmental aspects—United States—Juvenile literature. [1. Hazardous wastes—Environmental aspects. 2. Pollution.] I. Title. II. Series.
TD1050.E58G65　　1990　　　　　　　　　363.73'84—dc20　　　　　　　　90-36295　　CIP
ISBN 0-89686-542-8　　　　　　　　　　　　　　　　　　　　　　　　　　　　　　　　　AC

**Photo Credits**
Cover: Peter Arnold, Inc.: (Don Riepe)
Peter Arnold, Inc.: (Ray Pfortner) 4, 28
AP—Wide World Photos: 7, 16, 25
Devaney Stock Photos: (Claudio Ferrer) 10; 19
Earth Scenes: (Doug Wechsler) 13, 34
Greenpeace: (Sam Kittner) 22
Superstock: 31; (Timothy White) 37

Copyright © 1990 Crestwood House, Macmillan Publishing Company

All rights reserved. No part of this book may be reproduced or transmitted in any form or by any means, electronic or mechanical, including photocopying, recording, or by any information storage and retrieval system, without permission in writing from the Publisher.

Macmillan Publishing Company　　　　Collier Macmillan Canada, Inc.
866 Third Avenue　　　　　　　　　　　1200 Eglinton Avenue East
New York, NY 10022　　　　　　　　　　Suite 200
　　　　　　　　　　　　　　　　　　　Don Mills, Ontario M3C 3N1

**CRESTWOOD HOUSE**

Produced by Flying Fish Studio Incorporated

Printed in the United States of America

10 9 8 7 6 5 4 3 2

# CONTENTS

Warning from Love Canal..................................................5
Toxic Waste: What Is It?....................................................9
Chemical Dumps..............................................................12
Poison Air........................................................................15
Pesticides, Herbicides, and Other Chemicals...............17
Waste Oil..........................................................................24
Nuclear Power.................................................................24
Transportation: Dangers on the Highway.....................30
Household Hazards.........................................................32
Laws and Regulations.....................................................35
What Can You Do?..........................................................39
For More Information....................................................41
For Further Reading.......................................................43
Glossary............................................................................44
Index.................................................................................46

?????? CHEMICAL CO
?216 WEST 66TH PL
DOOR 24
CHICAGO ILL 60638

GROSS 271 LBS
TARE 21 LBS
NET 250 LBS

There was a strange stillness. The birds, for example—where had they gone? It was a spring without voices. On the mornings that had once throbbed with the dawn chorus of robins, catbirds, doves, jays, wrens, and scores of other bird voices, there was now no sound; only silence lay over the fields and woods and marshes.... No witchcraft, no enemy action had silenced the rebirth of new life in this stricken world. The people had done it themselves.

—Rachel Carson, *Silent Spring*

# WARNING FROM LOVE CANAL

Strange things began to happen in Love Canal in the 1970s. Six miles away from the famous Niagara Falls, Love Canal was an ordinary American town in northern New York. But something was happening—something horrible—that would soon set it apart from other towns.

*Toxic waste, buried in metal drums like this one, poisoned the town of Love Canal.*

Some of the children who played in the nearby creeks had trouble breathing at times. Other children had warts and headaches. Some pregnant women delivered dead babies. Other babies were born with defects.

Pets lost clumps of their fur. In certain areas, plants and trees were dying. A black sludge oozed through walls into basements.

People who lived in Love Canal were worried. They asked, then demanded, that tests be taken to find out what was causing the problems. The answer, when they finally learned it, was frightening.

Between 1942 and 1953, the Hooker Chemical & Plastics Corp. had dumped metal drums into an old canal in the town. The drums were filled with waste from pesticides the company made. In those 11 years, the company dumped 43.6 million pounds of waste in the canal. One of the chemicals in the waste was dioxin. Among the deadliest of all substances, dioxin has been linked to cancer and many other health problems.

After the canal was filled with waste, the company covered it over with soil. In 1953 Hooker Chemical sold the land to the town for $1. Planted with grass and trees, the land seemed to be a pleasant spot to build a school. Children who came to the school built there often played in the creeks nearby.

Below the ground, the metal drums slowly rusted. Leaking through the rusty holes, the toxic waste seeped into the soil and water. It filled the pools and creeks near the school where the children played.

Tests showed the waste had poisoned the area. It also threatened the health of the people living near the dump site. In 1978 President Jimmy Carter declared an emergency in Love Canal. During the next two years, more than a thousand families were moved out of the area.

Health problems caused by toxic waste forced the residents of Love Canal to move. Bulldozers flattened many of the houses near the dump, which is now covered by a mound of clay to prevent the dangerous chemicals from spreading.

People had to leave their neighbors and friends. Some were forced to give up clothes, toys, and books. One mother couldn't take her child's first pair of shoes with her because they had traces of poison on them.

In the years that followed, the state and federal governments spent $150 million on Love Canal. The money was used to pay families for the homes they had to leave, for tests, surveys, and cleanup.

Today Love Canal is a 40-acre mound of clay. The clay and a plastic cover seal the waste buried in the canal. Water poisoned by the waste is drained into a treatment plant.

Bulldozers flattened many of the homes nearest the dump. Others, boarded up and abandoned, are falling to the ground. Small traces of dioxin remain.

The families, once neighbors, now live all over the country. The government paid them for the homes they had to leave behind. But for some, there wasn't enough money to buy homes as nice as they had had before.

Most of their illnesses have gone away since the people moved from the area. But they still worry about cancer. Will it strike them or their children next year or in ten years?

Those who lost loved ones still grieve. One family, whose son played in the creeks, died from a strange kidney disease. Parents whose children were born with defects still struggle to help them. One girl was born deaf and with a hole in her heart. She and 1,327 other residents sued the company that dumped the waste at Love Canal. Hooker Chemical, now owned by Occidental Chemical Company, had to pay them $20 million. Even so, the company says it was not to blame. The courts still have not settled other suits in the case.

Love Canal—an ordinary American town—left behind a powerful lesson and a warning. If we do not heed that lesson, the problems of toxic waste will rise up again and again to destroy our towns and cities.

# TOXIC WASTE: WHAT IS IT?

Modern technology helps us live longer and more comfortable lives. Our homes are warm in winter, cool in summer. We eat foods from all over the world. Doctors save us from death with new drugs. Chemicals help stop disease, make crops grow faster, clean our drinking water, and make our engines run.

Chemical plants make the things we need to survive. They provide jobs for thousands of workers.

But there is a "down" side to modern technology: Chemicals that save our lives can also kill us. The chemicals used to make such useful things as plastics, pesticides, even paper and cloth, can be harmful, or toxic. Once the product is made, the leftover chemicals are thrown away. If not disposed of properly, the wastes can poison people and kill off trees, plants, and animals.

People exposed to toxic chemicals may have headaches, nausea, and rashes. More serious problems can also occur. Some

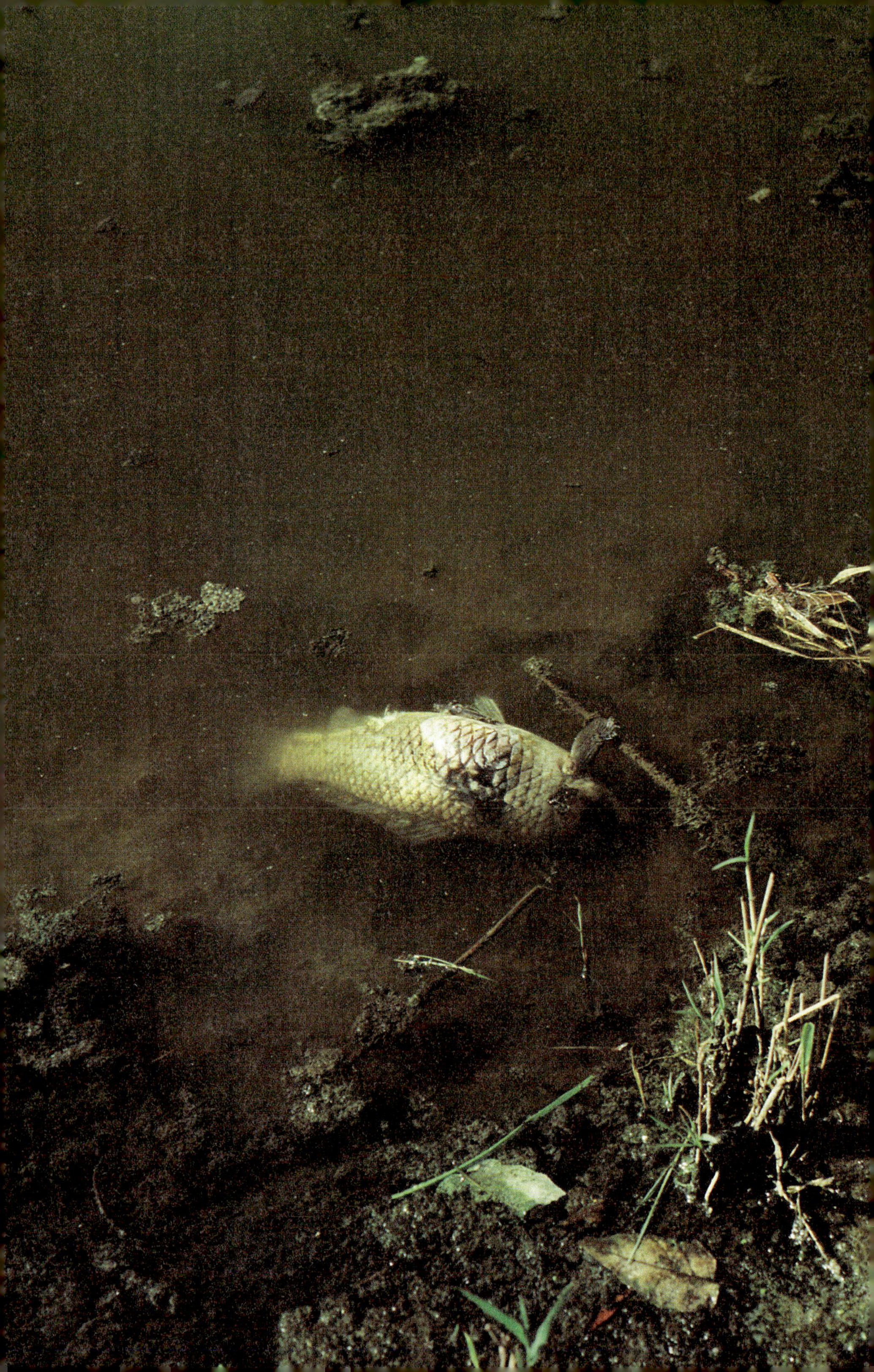

people have had burns from toxic wastes; some have had lung, kidney, or liver disease; others, cancer. Some have had babies with birth defects.

Each year the United States produces six billion tons of waste. Much of the waste is not toxic. About half is the remains of crops, plowed back into the ground. But some of the waste comes from industry. It can be very harmful to people and to the earth. Greenpeace, an environmental group, says American industry makes about one million pounds of toxic waste a minute.

## Through the Food Chain

Toxic waste can harm people even if they never touch it or feel it. Minamata Bay, a small fishing village in Japan, learned that sad lesson in 1952. In the streets, cats yowled wildly, then jumped into the sea to drown. Crows fell from the sky. People felt dizzy. They couldn't see or speak clearly. Some became blind. Others fell into comas or acted crazy.

A factory on the waterfront had dumped mercury into the water. The mercury had poisoned the fish. Then cats, birds, and people ate the poisoned fish. By 1971, 184 people had mercury poisoning in Minamata Bay. Eventually, 54 people died, and 26 were born with the disease.

There have been many other cases of poisons going through the food chain. The food chain is a series of living things that feed on other living things. For example, plants are eaten by insects, which are eaten by birds, which are eaten by people.

DDT, a toxic pesticide now banned, was once sprayed on grain. The grain was ground into meal and fed to chickens. People who ate the chickens' eggs also ate DDT. The toxin, or poison,

*Mercury poisoning destroys not only fish. It travels through the food chain, striking animals, birds, and people.*

was found in milk and butter produced by cows that ate the grain. Even human mothers' milk contained traces of DDT.

The amount of DDT increased with each link of the food chain. The chickens had more DDT than the grain. After eating the eggs, people had more DDT in their bodies than had the chickens.

## Toxins Everywhere

Toxins can be found almost everywhere. Most are made by chemical companies. Pulp and paper mills and the gasoline industry add their share. Hospitals produce wastes infected with disease germs. Power plants spew ash, while the local gas station throws away waste oil. Radiation leaks from nuclear power plants into the air.

Toxins are even present in our homes in the batteries, paints, and household cleansers we use every day. And thousands of new chemical compounds are made each year.

# CHEMICAL DUMPS

In the past, toxic waste was thrown away without much thought for safety. It was dumped in pits or on the ground and covered with dirt. Some wastes, like those at Love Canal, were stored in metal tanks that later rusted. Others were dumped into rivers or oceans. These toxic wastes become unseen time bombs, showing up years later to poison the earth.

*Ordinary household products like paints, cleansers, and bug sprays contain dangerous toxins. They must be disposed of properly to prevent the chemicals from polluting the environment.*

BRANDS' PAINT CO.
BALKAMP
EASY-OFF
LEMON SCENTED
MAKES OVEN CLEANING FAST & EASY
Sprayway
GLASS CLEANER
CAUTION
APPROVED BY GIRLING LIMITED
WEED-B-
ATLAS
PLASTI-WELD
FOR ABS PIPE & FITTINGS
ENERGINE
Spot Remover
jet-spray
CARBURETOR AND CHOKE CLEANER
PENNZOIL
SPRAYS AWAY FUEL SYSTEM AND VARNISH DEPOSITS
• Stops Squeaks
• Loosens Rusted
PARKS
100% Mineral Spirits
FLECTO
Varathane
LIQUID PLASTIC
CRYSTAL
All-Purpose Drain Opener
ATCO
1405
PENTA
WOOD
PRESERVATIVE
SEE CAUTIONS ON BACK PANEL
American Tar Company, Seattle
RED BAND
PAINTERS THINNER
Quality Guaranteed
Washable, Fade and Stain Resistant
Magicolor Latex
How to get ready for Painting
How to Paint with
Full 10 Year Warranty and Full Warranty at Time of Application
Weldwood
Plastic Resin
Glue
ATCO
Wet Surface
ASPHALT PLASTIC CEMENT
Glidden

Rain and snow filter through the earth, filling cracks and spaces in the rocks. This water below the surface is called groundwater. Half the people in the United States use groundwater to drink. Almost everyone who lives in the country drinks from a well or spring that taps into groundwater.

Groundwater is almost always cleaner than water above the surface. But it becomes polluted when toxic wastes are dumped in the area. Then rain washes the poisons into the water beneath the ground. The wastes can hurt crops and poison lakes and streams that are fed by groundwater. People in entire towns can no longer drink from their wells. They have to get water from other sources. In some places, like Love Canal, the pollution is so bad people can no longer live there.

The Rocky Mountain Arsenal in Denver, Colorado, is another example of the damage caused by leaking toxic waste. There, a company that made pesticides and products for chemical warfare stored waste in unlined ponds. The waste seeped into the groundwater. It polluted 64 wells used for watering crops and for supplying drinking water to people and livestock. The wells had to be abandoned.

When toxic wastes are dumped into rivers, the water becomes so dirty no one can fish or swim in it. Children and others who play along the banks become ill.

The federal government has set up a program called the Superfund to help clean up toxic wastes. The program also makes industries pay for cleaning up the toxic wastes they dump.

People now know dump sites have to be well sealed to stop leaks. In some cases, bacteria is used to eat up the wastes. The best solution, of course, is to prevent the problem. People are now pushing for laws that limit the use of the toxic chemicals. They also keep a close watch on how toxic wastes are disposed of in their towns.

# POISON AIR

Toxins can also be carried through the air. At some factories where harmful chemicals are used, toxins escape through smokestacks. These poisons may also be released into the air by accident if there is a fire or an explosion. Sometimes poisons escape when the people running the plant make a mistake. Safety systems that don't work the way they should are also to blame.

One of the worst accidents occurred in Bhopal, India. Union Carbide of India, Ltd., had made pesticides in Bhopal for 15 years. One of the chemicals used in the process was MIC (methyl isocyanate), a deadly gas. Just after midnight on December 3, 1984, more than 30 tons of methyl isocyanate escaped into the air.

Experts think water may have mixed with the methyl isocyanate, causing a chemical reaction. The pressure from this burst a safety valve. Other safety valves either were not turned on or were not working.

For almost two hours, a cloud of poison gas hung over Bhopal. A light wind carried it throughout the city. People's eyes burned, they choked on the poison, and they couldn't get their breath. Alarms warned of the danger several hours later. But for many it was too late. They had died in their sleep. Others who did escape became blind or died later.

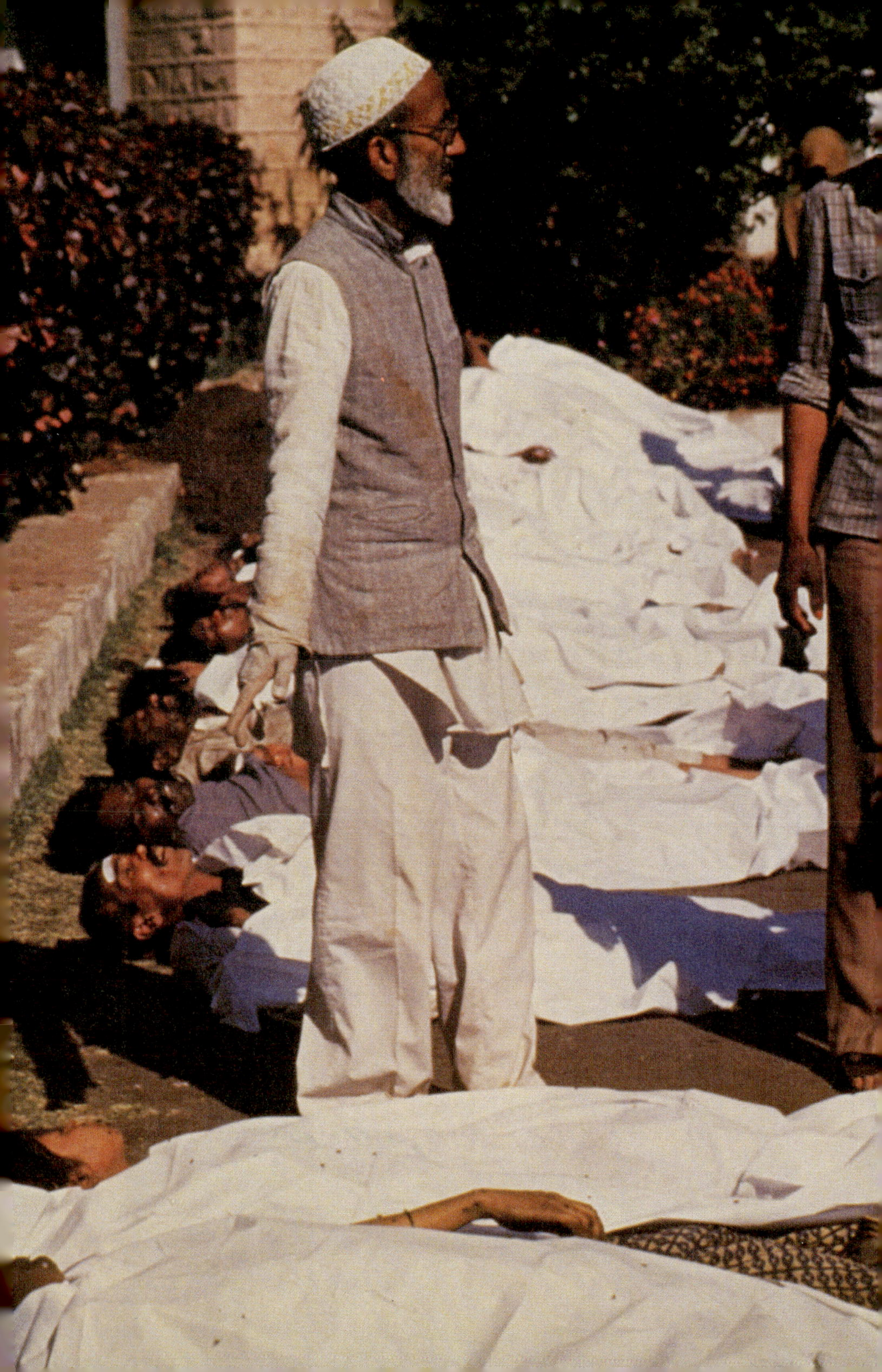

By the time the cloud had passed, 200,000 people had been exposed to the poison. Between 2,000 and 3,000 people died, and 100,000 were injured. Another 1,700 are expected to die by 1995.

Towns and cities in all parts of the world are now asking about the toxins used by companies in their area. They are working with companies to plan what to do if an accident occurs. New laws require that workers be trained well to handle equipment. They are also supposed to know what to do in emergencies. Plant personnel are being told to check equipment for safety.

Some towns ask companies for proof that their plants operate safely before they let them build new ones. Many towns also make sure factories using toxins are not built where a lot of people live.

# PESTICIDES, HERBICIDES, AND OTHER CHEMICALS

Among the most toxic chemicals are pesticides used to kill insects. About three billion pounds of pesticides are used in the United States each year. Farmers use them to protect their crops from destruction and disease.

Some experts argue that many pesticides do more harm than good. In Borneo mosquitoes gave people malaria, a disease that can be fatal. Pesticides were used to kill the mosquitoes. The

*Thousands died in Bhopal, India, when an explosion at a chemical plant sent deadly gas into the area.*

toxins worked, but they also killed cats and lizards. With no enemies to eat them, other types of insects and rats multiplied. They, too, spread disease to the people. Some insects even ate the thatched roofs of the homes in the village.

In some cases, chemical sprays lose their power over the insects they are designed to kill. At first the pesticides kill the bugs. But the toughest bugs live and have offspring that are not hurt by the spray. Scientists then have to make new sprays that are even more toxic.

People, on the other hand, can't fight off the chemicals. Each time they are exposed to the sprays, their bodies collect the poisons. They also eat traces of the toxins on sprayed food. Toxins can stay in people for years.

## DDT

DDT was created in 1874 by a German chemist. It was first used as a pesticide in 1939. Soon DDT was being used to help farmers win the war against insects.

It did indeed kill insects. But there were side effects. Scientists found DDT in the human body. Milk, crops, and soil also had traces of the poison. Experts found DDT in mothers' milk in 1951. By the beginning of the 1970s, Americans were thought to have 20 tons of DDT in their bodies. The pesticide has been linked to cancer and birth defects. It is not known whether there is a level of DDT that is safe for humans.

After eating plants with DDT on them, birds laid eggs with shells so thin they broke. Some birds, the brown pelican and the bald eagle, almost became extinct.

In 1969 people concerned about DDT took their case to the federal government. They wanted the toxin banned. But farmers

*Toxins have been found in the milk of cows that have eaten grass sprayed with chemicals or have breathed contaminated air.*

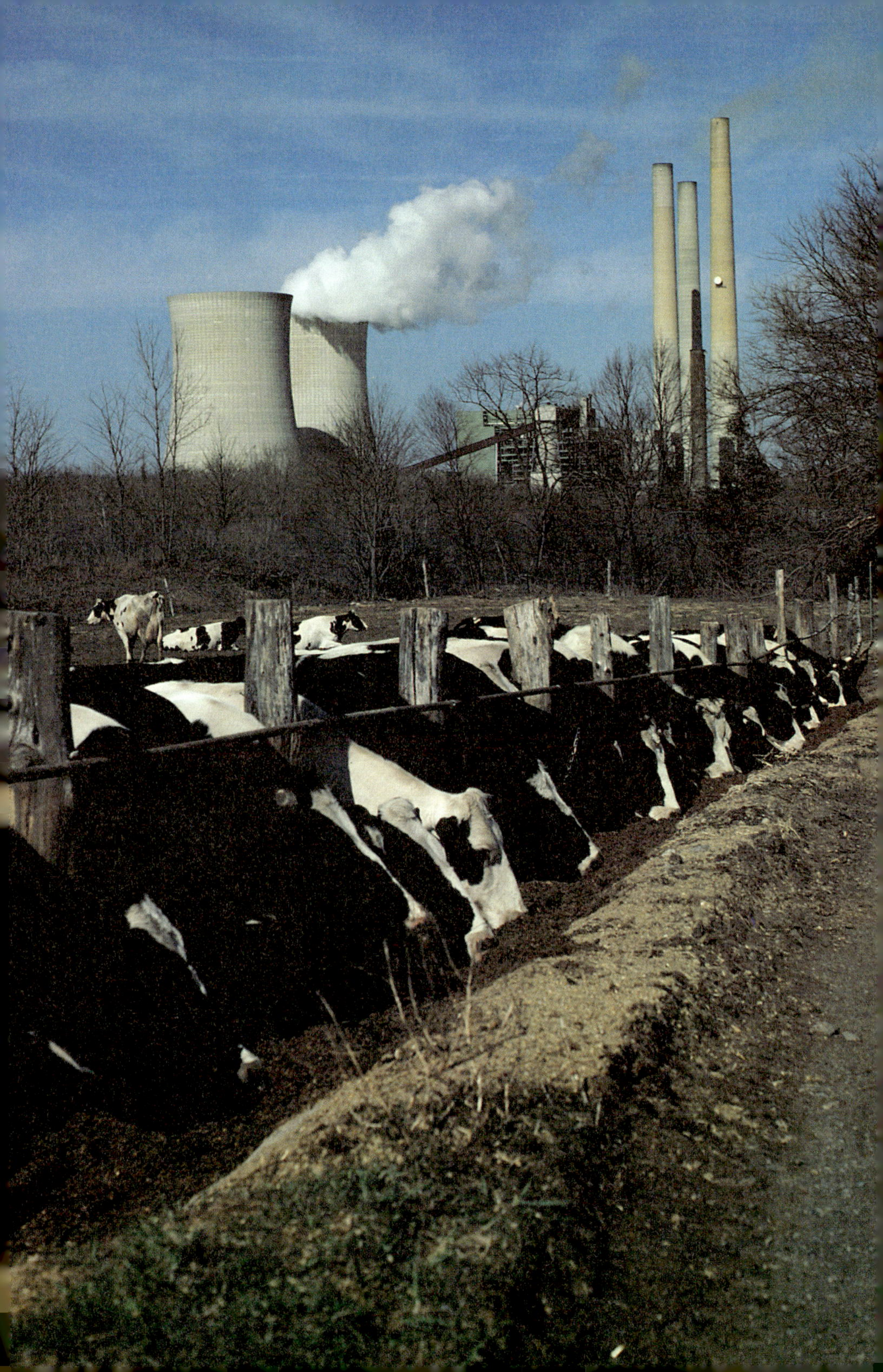

and the companies that made DDT wanted to keep using it. It took three years before DDT was banned for most uses.

## Herbicides

Other toxic chemicals, called herbicides, are used to kill weeds, trees, and bushes. Herbicides are sprayed on forests to kill unwanted trees, letting other trees grow faster. They are also used by farmers and home owners to kill weeds. Towns and cities use them to kill brush along roadways.

Dioxin, one of the deadliest chemicals known, is used in many herbicides. There are 75 types of dioxin. Some can be found in the treated wood used for decks and other outdoor projects, in pulp and paper mills, and in certain shampoos and paint.

People become exposed to dioxin by breathing it or touching plants sprayed with it. Dioxin has also been found in milk and fish in areas where the poison has been sprayed or spilled.

In Seveso, Italy, 739 people had to move when an explosion sprayed dioxin into the air. Children became sick and sores appeared on their skin. Others had damaged livers and blurred vision. One year later, women in the area had reported 51 miscarriages.

At the time of the blast, dead birds fell from the sky and pets died. After a year, 81,000 animals had died or had to be killed. Dioxin was found in 124 schools in the area.

The company that made the pesticide agreed to pay $109 million to the people in the town. Some may not be able to go back home for half a century because of the poisons there.

Dioxin was used in Agent Orange, which was sprayed during the Vietnam War to destroy jungles and farms. The spray was so toxic it could turn a ten-mile stretch of trees into a wasteland in a few days. It has since been banned.

Veterans of the war who were exposed to Agent Orange have reported cancers and other diseases. Some of their children have been born with defects.

## PCBs

The story of PCBs follows the same course as DDT. (PCB is short for polychlorinated biphenyl.) Used widely in many products, PCBs began to show up in humans, fish, and water. Like DDT, they have been linked to cancer and birth defects.

From the beginning, in 1930, PCBs caused sores on the skin of workers making them. Since then 1.5 billion pounds of PCBs have been made. They have been used mainly as fluids to transfer heat in electric transformers. PCBs have also been used in copy paper, paints, inks, and dyes.

PCBs do not break down. Once in the environment, they stay there. Traces of the toxins have shown up in polar bears in the Arctic. They have been found in mothers' milk around the globe.

Even though companies were banned from making PCBs in 1979, they are still a problem. Almost 760 million pounds of PCBs are still in use. Another 290 million pounds are in dumps and landfills, and 150 million pounds are in the air, soil, and water.

As with DDT, no one knows what levels of PCBs are safe for humans.

New pesticides are tested before they can be sold in the United States. But for some people, the laws and rules have come too late. Sometimes the laws are passed only after people have been hurt. It is often hard to prove that health problems are caused by the

*Waste oil dumped in streams like this can contaminate an entire area.*

toxins. Some diseases, such as certain forms of cancer, take years to appear.

The government can stop the use of a dangerous pesticide. But it can take many years to get it off the market. Scientist Rachel Carson warned about DDT in 1962 in her book *Silent Spring*. But DDT wasn't banned until ten years later. By that time, traces of DDT were found in about 97 percent of all humans tested. The amount of DDT in humans has gone down since it was banned.

The federal government is testing 600 chemicals in 25,000 pesticides for safety. That review won't be done until 1997. To be safe, some people spray their gardens and crops only with natural sprays. Gardeners who worry about toxins pull their weeds by hand.

People in some areas use birds or insects to kill harmful insects. For example, dragonflies have been shipped into swampy areas to eat mosquitoes. Researchers are working to create plants that don't need pesticides to survive.

People who think toxins are dangerous are asking woodland owners to cut back on the sprays they use. They also want sprayers to aim with care, away from people and homes. And they ask that spraying be stopped when wind or rain will spread the chemicals to other areas.

The best way to protect against toxins is to prohibit the most harmful ones. Some people would like to see all but the most needed toxins banned forever.

# WASTE OIL

Underground tanks have been used for years to store wastes, oil, and other substances. Many were made of steel and are now old and rusting. Experts think there may be five to six million tanks buried underground. Of those, about two million are thought to be leaking. There are also thousands of miles of pipes beneath the ground, many of which are leaking, too.

The tanks leak into groundwater and wells. Leaks may also cause fires and explosions. Lighter than water, gas floats on top of groundwater. It flows into basements and sewers, where fumes collect. In Pennsylvania, a woman's house exploded when gas fumes collected in the basement. An underground gas tank was found nearby.

Waste oil caused other problems in Times Beach, Missouri. People there had to leave their homes after the soil and groundwater were poisoned by waste oil. The oil, mixed with dioxin, had been used on the roads in the town.

New laws require that tanks and pipelines be tested for leaks. Leaking tanks have to be dug up and the area sealed to stop the pollution.

# NUCLEAR POWER

Nuclear power has been put forth by some people as the answer to the world's energy needs. Its supporters say it helps cut down on air pollution caused by oil, coal, and wood used for fuel.

*The accident at Three Mile Island awoke people to the dangers of nuclear power.*

Nuclear power is produced by splitting atoms. It was first used to make bombs during World War II. After the war, the United States government used nuclear power to produce energy. By the late 1980s, there were more than 110 nuclear power plants in the United States.

The plants create power by splitting uranium or thorium atoms. The splitting of the atoms gives off heat. That in turn heats water at the plant. The steam produced is used to make electricity.

The fuel—uranium or thorium—is packed in fuel rods in the core of the plant. If for some reason the fuel overheats, it can melt the fuel rods. This meltdown would allow radioactive gases to escape.

To stop the gases from escaping to the outside air, the plant is put inside a second building. A cooling system and filters keep the gases inside.

Unfortunately, the safety measures don't always work.

## Three Mile Island

On March 28, 1979, a nuclear power plant at Three Mile Island in Middletown, Pennsylvania, had a partial meltdown. The accident released radioactive gases into the air. It also badly damaged the plant. Pregnant women and children were told to leave the area. The accident was blamed on machines that weren't working right and on human error.

There is no record of any deaths directly caused by the accident. But some experts say the accident was responsible for the deaths of several babies. They predict that there will be more cases of cancer in the area.

Before the accident, most people believed nuclear power plants were safe. The meltdown at Three Mile Island made many wonder if nuclear power was worth the risk.

## Chernobyl

A much worse accident happened on April 26, 1986, at Chernobyl in the Soviet Union. A fire in the nuclear power plant caused an explosion. It killed 31 people and sent radioactive gases all the way to Europe. The fire burned for five days. The explosion occurred while safety systems in the plant were shut down for a test. Within minutes, the fire was out of control. The explosion ripped open the core of the plant.

Doctors treated 200 people for radiation exposure. They believe 5,000 to 40,000 people will die of cancer over the next 70 years because of the blast.

More than 135,000 people had to move from the area. Twenty-seven towns were abandoned forever. Gases from the plant were found in rainwater in England. Poland had to ban its milk. Other countries destroyed crops poisoned by the gases. Experts estimate the blast caused $2.7 billion of damage.

## Nuclear Waste

Nuclear power plants create two kinds of waste: high-level and low-level radioactive nuclear waste. Radioactive matter gives off toxic gases that cause cancer or death in high doses. High-level waste comes from the used fuel, which stays toxic for hundreds of thousands of years. The used pipes, filters, and other hardware in

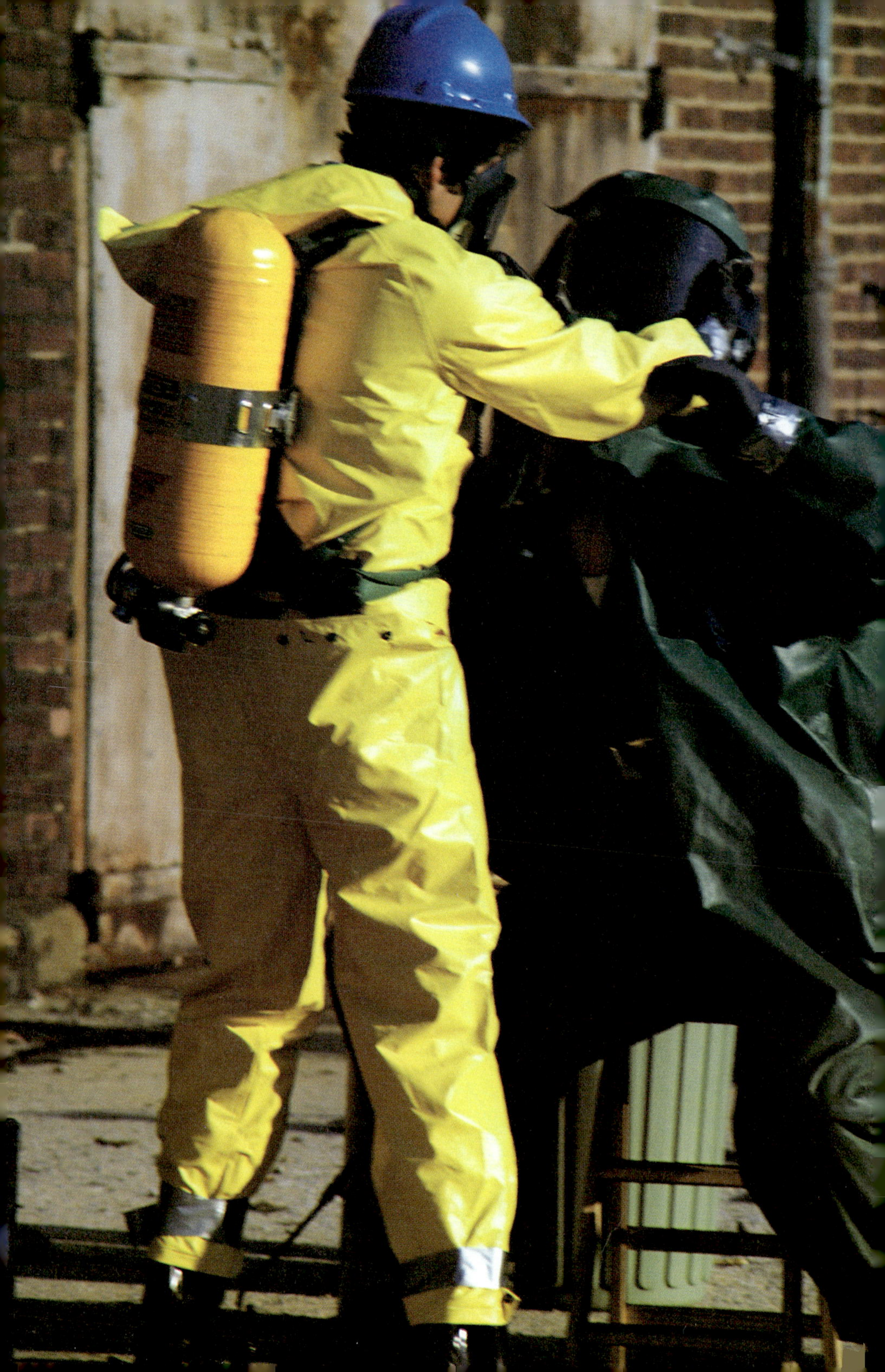

the plant are low-level waste. In fact the whole plant, built to last only 40 years, becomes low-level waste. Hospitals also produce low-level waste from such things as X rays.

Each nuclear power plant makes about 33 tons of high-level waste a year. Plants have already made a total of about 13,775 tons of the hot waste. Over four million cubic yards of low-level waste are stored at six dumps. Three of the dumps are now closed. The other three are in Washington, South Carolina, and Nevada.

So far, no one has found a good way to get rid of the waste. Low-level wastes, stored in trenches, have poisoned nearby soil and water. Most high-level waste is kept in pools at power plants. There it stays until someone finds a way to store it safely.

Some people suggest that the wastes be made into a solid block. Then the block could be sealed in glass and buried deep in the ground. It could also be coated with metal for extra safety.

Other people think the earth may shift and damage the blocks of waste. Then the gases, still toxic hundreds of years later, would escape.

Most accidents at nuclear power plants have occurred partly because someone made a mistake. Workers need to be trained, tested, and taught safety measures. Equipment should be checked regularly. Plants should be built away from cities and in places not likely to have earthquakes, floods, or windstorms. Experts should check to make sure the plants are built properly. All safety systems should be working.

Towns and cities near nuclear power plants must plan what to do if an accident occurs. People need to be told of a leak at once and moved out of the area if necessary.

Trucks and trains carrying nuclear matter should be checked for safety. Waste should be stored in very secure containers.

*People who work with toxic chemicals must wear special protective gear.*

Some people think nuclear power plants should be shut down because they are so dangerous. Even small leaks can increase people's risk of developing cancer. A major leak could kill thousands. Opponents of nuclear energy say there is no safe way to store nuclear waste because it stays toxic for thousands of years. Plutonium, a nuclear fuel, can be deadly for up to 250,000 years.

# TRANSPORTATION: DANGERS ON THE HIGHWAY

Toxins and toxic wastes must be carried over roads and rails, some for long distances. In an accident, spills can pollute a large area. This could be tragic if nuclear wastes escaped. Such spills would continue to pollute the area for thousands of years.

Some spills are not accidental. One company paid a man $75,000 to get rid of 31,000 gallons of waste oil. The oil contained PCBs. John Burns and his two sons dumped the oil along 210 miles of roads in North Carolina. As the poisons spread, people in the area suffered headaches, their eyes burned, their throats were sore. They were warned not to eat the livestock or crops raised along the route. Some people stopped using their wells.

Burns was arrested. But four years after the dumping, much of the area still was poisoned.

*A workman wearing a protective mask removes asbestos from a house. Once used extensively as insulation, asbestos has been found to cause cancer and lung disease.*

Many people want stricter laws to be passed to stop illegal dumping. They want those moving toxic waste to take the safest routes and avoid areas with many people. They want trucks and railcars carrying toxic wastes carefully checked for safety.

When spills do occur, experts can prevent disaster. For example, they know that water sprayed on the roads can spread toxins to nearby streams and groundwater. That's what happened near Wheeling, West Virginia, when a truck carrying 40,000 pounds of acid crashed. The weather was bad and toxic fumes began to rise and spread. Money from the Superfund was used to clean up the spill before it could do much damage.

# HOUSEHOLD HAZARDS

Though most toxic wastes are created by industry, toxins can be found in almost every home.

## Asbestos

Asbestos at one time was used to insulate homes and buildings against the cold. But when it gets old, it crumbles. Small asbestos fibers pass into the air and stick in people's lungs. This can cause lung cancer and other lung diseases. Though no longer used in buildings, asbestos is still found in many old structures.

A law passed in 1986 requires all school officials to find out if asbestos was used in their buildings. Federal grants and loans help schools pay for removing asbestos. Trained workers, dressed in masks and special clothing, now remove the asbestos from schools and public buildings, as well as from many homes.

## Radon

Radon is a colorless, odorless gas that exists in nature. It is formed when radioactive radium decays. Radon is present in small amounts in almost all parts of the country. In some areas, high amounts of radon are found. It can enter a home through cracks in the foundation or through water from a well that contains radon.

People who breathe too much radon can get lung cancer and other lung problems. The effect it has on other parts of the body is not known. People who mine uranium are most likely to suffer health problems from radon. People working near uranium need to wear masks and gear to protect themselves.

There are tests to find out if there is too much radon gas in homes and other buildings. If the amount of radon is high, people may have to seal off their basements and stop drinking from wells that have radon in them.

## Household Chemicals

Chemicals are used in all sorts of household goods. When these are thrown away, they can pollute the environment if they are not handled properly. Among toxic products found in homes are drain and oven cleaners, polishes, old medicines, batteries, paint thinners, and pesticides.

*Some communities hold waste collection drives so that people can safely dispose of any hazardous products they may have in their homes.*

In some states, companies selling toxins for household use must have a permit. They also have to label each product as toxic. States and towns have cleanup days to collect toxic waste people have in their homes. Such wastes should never be poured down the drain, burned, or spread on the lawn.

# LAWS AND REGULATIONS

Love Canal alerted the nation to the dangers of toxic waste. In 1980 the U.S. Congress created the Superfund. The new law set aside $1.6 billion to help clean up toxic waste dumps. It also instructed the Environmental Protection Agency (EPA) to find those who dumped the toxic waste and get them to help clean it up.

The EPA is the federal agency that was formed to control and prevent pollution. It enforces rules on toxic and other wastes, pesticides, water, air, and radioactive substances.

In the past ten years, the EPA has found 30,000 sites that may be the source of toxins. Of those, 1,177 have been placed on the EPA's list for cleanup. To help pay for the cleanup, a new law has raised the Superfund to $8.5 billion. Even so, the money will most likely pay for the cleanup of only about 400 sites.

The EPA also seeks money from those who dumped the wastes. Some states, such as Pennsylvania and Connecticut, have their own Superfund laws to help pay the cleanup costs.

Other laws help protect the environment. In addition to the Superfund, federal laws include:

• The National Environmental Policy Act (1969). Under this act, all federal agencies must show how their projects will affect the environment.

• The Occupational Safety and Health Act (1970). OSHA sets rules to protect workers from being hurt on the job. This includes rules on the handling of toxic chemicals.

• The Clean Air Act (1970). This law ordered states to set limits for air pollution by 1975. Many states didn't meet the deadline, and the dates were extended in 1977. Congress is thinking of making this law stricter.

• The Federal Insecticide, Fungicide, and Rodenticide Act (1972). This law gives the federal government control over the sale and use of pesticides. Pesticides must be registered with the EPA. Their labels must tell how to use the toxins properly.

• The Safe Drinking Water Act (1974). This act was passed to make sure water is safe to drink. Anyone who provides water to the public has to meet certain standards.

• The Toxic Substances Control Act (1976). This law requires that all new chemicals be tested to see if they are toxic. Chemicals already in use may also be tested under this law if they are thought to be hazardous.

• The Resource Conservation and Recovery Act (1976). This law requires that hazardous wastes be disposed of safely. It also says that anyone who creates or handles such waste must tell where it came from and how and where it was discarded.

• The Clean Water Act (1977). This law makes it illegal to dump toxic wastes into waters without having a permit. It also provides money for sewage treatment plants.

*When people bring paper and other products to recycling stations like this one, they help prevent toxic waste from polluting the environment.*

• The Superfund Amendments and Reauthorization Act (1986). These changes to the Superfund law gave the EPA more power to get polluters to clean up their waste. It set aside $8.5 billion for the cleanup program. An additional $500 million was set aside for cleaning up leaks from underground tanks.

• The Emergency Preparedness and Community Right-to-Know Act (1986). Congress passed this law to help protect the public during accidents with toxic wastes and chemicals. Under the law, state and local groups have to set up plans for what to do in an accident involving dangerous chemicals. The law also requires companies to tell the groups when toxins are released by accident. The companies must tell fire departments, rescue workers, and the state and local groups about the toxic chemicals they use.

State and local governments have their own laws and rules governing toxic waste. In 1989 Massachusetts and Oregon became the first two states in the nation to pass laws aimed at reducing the use of toxins. Under these laws, companies and others who use toxic chemicals must report what they use. They must also make plans to reduce the amounts they use.

On the local level, towns and cities can set rules telling industries where they can build their plants. These zones can be set aside for industry only, away from people's homes. Planning boards can look over companies' plans and decide whether to allow them to build in their communities.

# WHAT CAN YOU DO?

In 1988, nine-year-old Melissa Poe saw a TV show about a world destroyed by pollution. Frightened, she wondered what she could do to help clean up the world. But what could a nine-year-old girl from Tennessee do?

She decided to write to the president. When he didn't respond to her pleas about pollution, she wrote to other people. Melissa convinced ad agencies in her state to help. They put up a big sign asking people to stop pollution. She formed a group of students at her school to fight pollution. Instead of throwing things away, they try to use them again. They pitch in to clean up their town and tell others about their cause.

Melissa wrote another letter that spread her message even further. After hearing from Melissa, the producers of the *Today Show* invited her to tell her story to the nation. Television viewers around the country heard how she was fighting pollution.

Other people are doing their part. Lois Gibbs and her neighbors at Love Canal talked to reporters, paid for studies, and wrote letters. They held demonstrations and spoke at public meetings. Finally they pushed public officials to do something about the dump in their town. With the lessons she learned from the Love Canal fight, Gibbs formed her own group, Citizens' Clearinghouse for Hazardous Wastes, Inc. It helps other people fight against toxic waste in their towns.

Other nonprofit groups, such as the United States Public Interest Research Group, do research and lobby for laws to protect the environment. All states and many towns and cities have their own clubs and groups. They all need money and volunteers to help in the fight against pollution.

What can *you* do?

- Ask speakers to talk to your class about toxic waste.
- Try to use products that don't have toxins.
- Do not pour toxic wastes down the drain or onto the ground.
- Cut down on the amount of things you throw away. (Use a glass instead of a Styrofoam or plastic cup, for example.)
- Recycle as much as you can.
- Take part in community cleanup days.
- Read labels and follow directions on how to use products and how to dispose of them.
- Write to state and federal legislators in support of laws that will help protect the environment.
- Join groups working to fight pollution.

Everyone can do something to help in the fight against toxic waste. All over the country and the world, neighbors are uniting to keep their communities safe and clean.

# FOR MORE INFORMATION

For more information on toxic waste and environmental issues, you can write or call the following groups:

American Cancer Society
261 Madison Avenue
New York, NY 10016
(212) 599-3600

American Lung Association
1740 Broadway
New York, NY 10019-4374
(212) 315-8700

Citizens' Clearinghouse for Hazardous Wastes, Inc.
PO Box 926
Arlington, VA 22216
(703) 276-7070

Environmental and Occupational Health Sciences Institute
675 Hoes Lane
Piscataway, NJ 08854-5635
(201) 463-4828

Environmental Defense Fund
257 Park Avenue South
New York, NY 10010
(212) 505-2100

National Institute for Chemical Studies
2300 MacCorkle Avenue SE
Charleston, WV 25304
(304) 346-6264

Pennsylvania Alliance for Environmental Education
601 Orchid Place
Emmaus, PA 18049
(215) 967-PAEE

U.S. Department of Health and Human Services
Public Health Service
Centers for Disease Control
Atlanta, GA 30333

U.S. Environmental Protection Agency
401 M Street SW
Washington, DC 20460
(202) 382-5926

U.S. Public Interest Research Groups
National Association of State PIRGs
215 Pennsylvania Avenue SE
Washington, DC 20003
(202) 546-9707

You may also want to contact your representative or senator for information on laws and bills before Congress concerning the environment.

# FOR FURTHER READING

Berger, Melvin. *Hazardous Substances, a Reference.* Hillside, NJ: Enslow Publishing, 1986.

Bright, Michael. *Pollution and Wildlife.* New York: Gloucester Press, 1987.

Gay, Kathlyn. *Silent Killers: Radon and Other Hazards.* New York: Franklin Watts, 1988.

Halacy, Daniel Stephen. *Now or Never: The Fight Against Pollution.* New York: Four Winds Press, 1971.

Hawkes, Nigel. *Nuclear Safety.* New York: Gloucester Press, 1987.

Kiefer, Irene. *Nuclear Energy at the Crossroads.* New York: Atheneum, 1982.

———. *Poisoned Land: The Problems of Hazardous Waste.* New York: Atheneum, 1981.

Stwertka, Albert and Eve. *Industrial Pollution: Poisoning Our Planet.* New York: Franklin Watts, 1981.

Zipko, Stephen J. *Toxic Threat: How Hazardous Substances Poison Our Lives.* New York: J. Messner, 1986.

# GLOSSARY

**Agent Orange** *Toxic spray used to kill jungles and farmland in Vietnam during the war.*
**asbestos** *Fibers used to insulate homes and buildings; can cause lung cancer and other lung diseases.*
**Bhopal, India** *Site of accident where 200,000 people were poisoned by MIC, 2,000 to 3,000 of whom died.*
**Carson, Rachel** *Scientist who wrote the book* Silent Spring *to warn against DDT and other pesticides.*
**Chernobyl** *Site of nuclear power plant in the Soviet Union that exploded and sent radioactive gases all the way to Europe.*
**DDT** *A pesticide now banned.*
**dioxin** *One of the deadliest chemicals, used to make pesticides.*
**Environmental Protection Agency (EPA)** *Federal agency formed to control and prevent pollution.*
**food chain** *A series of living things that feed on other living things and then themselves become food. For example, spiders feed on flies, birds feed on spiders, people feed on birds. Pesticides become more concentrated with each step up the food chain. For example, chickens eating sprayed alfalfa would contain a higher amount of pesticides than the alfalfa; eggs laid by the chickens would have an even higher amount; and the people who ate the eggs would have the highest amount of all.*
**groundwater** *Water that flows under the earth's surface. It is used by many for drinking water.*
**Love Canal** *A town in northern New York State that had to be abandoned because of toxic waste buried there.*
**meltdown** *When the fuel in a nuclear plant overheats and melts the fuel rods (where the fuel is stored).*
**MIC** *Methyl isocyanate, a deadly gas used to make pesticides.*

**Minamata Bay** *A small fishing village in Japan where the people were poisoned by mercury in the fish.*

**PCB** *Polychlorinated biphenyl, a toxic chemical used in electric transformers, copy paper, paints, and other products.*

**radon** *A colorless, odorless gas formed when radioactive radium decays; can cause lung cancer and other lung problems.*

**Rocky Mountain Arsenal** *A site in Denver, Colorado, poisoned by waste from pesticides and chemical warfare products.*

**Seveso, Italy** *Site of an explosion that sprayed a pesticide in the air and forced more than 700 people to move from their homes.*

**Superfund** *A fund set up by Congress to help pay for cleanup of toxic waste.*

**thorium** *A nuclear fuel.*

**Three Mile Island** *In Pennsylvania, site of the worst nuclear power plant accident in the United States.*

**toxic** *Harmful or poisonous.*

**toxin** *Poison.*

**uranium** *A nuclear fuel.*

# INDEX

Agent Orange 20, 21
asbestos 32, 33

Bhopal, India 15, 17
Borneo 17
Burns, John 30

Carson, Rachel 5, 23
Carter, President Jimmy 6
chemical dumps 14, 21
chemicals 6, 9, 12, 14, 15, 18, 20, 23, 33, 36, 38
Chernobyl 27
Citizens' Clearinghouse for Hazardous Wastes, Inc. 39
Clean Air Act 36
Clean Water Act 36

DDT 11, 12, 18, 20, 21, 23
dioxin 6, 8, 20, 24

Emergency Preparedness and Community Right-to-Know Act 38
Environmental Protection Agency (EPA) 35, 36, 38

Federal Insecticide, Fungicide, and Rodenticide Act 36
food chain 11, 12

Gibbs, Lois 39
Greenpeace 11
groundwater 14, 24, 32

herbicides 20
Hooker Chemical & Plastics Corp. 6, 8

Love Canal 5, 6, 7, 8, 9, 12, 14, 35, 39

meltdown 26, 27
mercury poisoning 11
MIC 15
Middletown, Pennsylvania 26
Minamata Bay 11

National Environmental Policy Act 36
nuclear power 24, 25, 26, 27, 29, 30

Occidental Chemical Co. 8
Occupational Safety and Health Act (OSHA) 36

PCBs 21, 30
pesticides 9, 11, 14, 15, 17, 18, 20, 21, 33, 35, 36
plutonium 30
Poe, Melissa 39

radon 33
Resource Conservation and Recovery Act 36
Rocky Mountain Arsenal 14

Safe Drinking Water Act 36
Seveso, Italy 20
*Silent Spring* 5, 23
Superfund 14, 32, 35, 36, 38

thorium 26
Three Mile Island 26, 27
Times Beach, Missouri 24
*Today Show* 39
Toxic Substances Control Act 36
toxic waste 6, 9, 11, 12, 14, 15, 30, 32, 35, 36, 38, 39, 40
toxins 11, 12, 15, 17, 18, 21, 23, 30, 32, 35, 36, 38, 40

Union Carbide of India, Ltd. 15
United States Public Interest Research Group 39
uranium 26, 33

Vietnam War 20

Wheeling, West Virginia 32